Eccentric Orbits

An Anthology of Sci-Fi Poetry
Volume 1

ISBN: 978-1-9992160-6-1
Dimensionfold Publishing
Anthology published April 2020
Prince George BC CAN

All works retain the original copyrights of their authors

Cover art by Ian Bristow

Contents

Foreword	1
The Jellyfish - Lee Garratt	3
Pioneer - Stephanie Barr	5
Under the Terms of Victory - Lee Garratt	8
Warp Bubble - Wendy Van Camp	10
Missing Matter - Kimberly Nugent	11
Alcubierre Metric - Wendy Van Camp	12
Warp Dreams - Wendy Van Camp	13
Rewriting the Rules - Kimberly Nugent	14
Faster Than Light - Wendy Van Camp	15
Hello - Kimberly Nugent	16
A Sun's Death - Kimberly Nugent	17
Singularity - Kimberly Nugent	18
Columbia - R. C. Larlham	19
Starship Troopers - Lee Garratt	20
Where We Go, They Follow	22
- Kimberly Nugent	22
Catz and Dogz: Godz and Quantum Chaos - R. C. Larlham	23
Witness - Thomas Van Horn	25
Chores - Kimberly Nugent	40
Time Traveller – Andrew Burton	41

Walkabout In Space - RC Larlham	43
O My Princess - Mike Van Horn	46
Transmissions from Trillig - Lee Garratt	47
My Best Friend Is Gone - Mike Van Horn	48
Formation's Song - Kimberly Nugent	50
The Experiment - Deborah L. Kelly	51
I Have Tasted the Infinite - Mike Van Horn	52
Forbidden Pictures; chapter three - Ken Goudsward	53
The Twelfth Planet: Nibiru - Deborah L. Kelly	54
Program - Ken Goudsward	56
Forever to Infinity - Mike Van Horn	57
Alexa Said - Jane Jago	58
The Flash - Erin J. Bauman	59
Colony - Lee Garratt	60
Anthem to a New World - Mike Van Horn	61
The Cylon Poem - Erin J. Bauman	64
Intrinsic Connection - Deborah L. Kelly	65
Worlds away - Andrew Burton	66
An Interstellar Legend - Kimberly Nugent	67

Foreword

By Wendy Van Camp

One of the reasons why I enjoy reading science fiction is the translation of ideas of today that demonstrate how they may be in our future. Concepts that are a mere glimmer in the eye of the poet can inspire our engineers and entrepreneurs into shaping our lives in ways that otherwise we might never have experienced.

In your hands is an anthology devoted to this science fiction spirit of tomorrow. The poets represented in this work are gathered from various artistic organizations to create a unique volume allowing you that superlative glimpse into various futures. Many different forms of poetry are represented, from humble science fiction themed haiku to free verse. All will invite you to speculate and wonder about humanity's eventualities.

Come join us on this exciting journey of poetic expression.

The Jellyfish - Lee Garratt

Wave borne
the jellyfish hangs, and drifts
in the pulsing abyss
of the moon drunk sea.

As an astronaut
loose from his cord
falls away from the light,
forever into the dark.

If they are conscious they must be mad.
No reason can hold here,
where infantile beasts hoot
and whistle on their endless, insane
wanderings.

Then, by some absurd chance in this eternity of space,
to hit the awful rock,
betrayed, all rules broken,
dragged onto the sand and left,
to dim and die
in the air,
where one must support one's own weight.

As we all must, as we come rushing up
for air,
each morning on waking,
Our dreams already floating away,
forever into infinite space.

In the morning on the damp margin of the beach that shrinks from the cold sea,
A child finds a glob of matter a hand across.
What dreams may come.

Pioneer - Stephanie Barr

Silent on the nascent grass,
She wandered on the hill,
A gas tank on her slender back;
Her breathing broke the still.
Her eyes weren't on the grass though
But fastened on the sky.
She wondered always if they'd come
And if she'd ever fly.

The stars were silent, cold and still,
No promise would they hold.
She shivered in the tiny breeze
And hurried from the cold.
She set her tank up to recharge
And put her mask away.
Inside the air was warm and rich.
She shivered just the same.

Her footsteps sounded in the halls once built
For a full ten thousand men.
But there was naught but echoes now
To say they'd ever been.
She remembered laughter,
Children running in the halls.
Ordered shouts and quiet murmurs,
Friendly waves and calls.

Ten thousand souls to colonize
This nearly-lifeless rock.

That nearly-lifeless aspect
Was what gave them all a shock.
A virus no one thought could be
Brought in from scoutabout.
That spread like wildfire through them
Rotting from the inside out.

The laughter turned to screaming,
To whimpers, groans of pain
But living with the silence made her
Miss those sounds again.
No one, young or old, was spared,
No one but Malu.
Malu who burned their corpses
For that's all that she could do.

She'd tried to nurse, tried to save them,
Comfort their last days,
But she'd been trained a fighter
And didn't have the ways.
They pled with her to save them.
All she could do was cry.
And haul their corpses, one by one,
And wait her turn to die.

Ten thousand through the airlock
And burned to light the sky
Then trudged back to the empty halls
And wait her turn to die.
But Malu lived and did the work
Ten thousand came to do.
She tended fields and nurtured stock
And then, when that was through,

She strapped on tanks and wandered
Over many an empty hill
And stared into a star-filled sky
She felt cold and empty still.
Before she trudges back inside
This settlement she calls home.
And wonders if she'll ever be
Anything but alone.

Under the Terms of Victory - Lee Garratt

and in the name of peace,
planets are being destroyed.
Asteroid belts grow
and bright flares suddenly
erupt in the sky above.
We gaze up for a moment
then turn back to our drinks,
a little abashed.

I stand on the deck
as we approach one of the vanquished worlds.
Insignificant.
Weak.
Laser cannons primed,
we notice vast white flags that,
by some massive effort of labour and organisation,
were draped over the highest peaks,
the nations' Capitol,
on their deserts.
Some of the officers sniggered,
some were silent,
but we blasted the planet just the same.

I didn't say,
didn't want to intrude
that it was my home planet below
a poor place from long ago.
I remember the day I left,
looking back at my mother
waving a white handkerchief.
I watched till she disappeared.

Warp Bubble - Wendy Van Camp

as space contracts ahead
we travel without moving
no time dilation

Missing Matter - Kimberly Nugent

stars and gas
unexpectedly lightweight
missing scaffolding
unfolding space-time
dark matter deficiency

Alcubierre Metric - Wendy Van Camp

inside warp bubble
relativistic effects
never will apply

Warp Dreams - Wendy Van Camp

warp speed is a joke
stretch the fabric of spacetime
who is laughing now?

Rewriting the Rules - Kimberly Nugent

dark matter
astronomers in heated debate
modified gravity

Faster Than Light - Wendy Van Camp

exoplanets beckon
Alcubierre's equations
allow visitation

Hello - Kimberly Nugent

jump of the needle
repeating fast radio burst
ghosts from Auriga

A Sun's Death - Kimberly Nugent

exhausting fuel supply
peculiar cosmic fluctuation
color collapse into white

Singularity - Kimberly Nugent

swirl into decay
tidal forces increase the pull
star black death

Columbia - R. C. Larlham

O God – we mourn again
Our fallen seekers of the stars.
Just days beyond remembrance of the others,
Bright expanding fire set free these souls
From lightspeed's mundane grip,
To seek their joy among the suns.

I would have gone – could I have done.
In fact, I have, a thousand times
With Heinlein, Asimov, von Braun,
And others, all who knew before we dreamed
That Space was but another sea
Like those we've sailed before.

Danger's always there – and death, we know.
But we must bravely go to find new lands,
Where no man's foot has set before.
And after Luna, Mars, Europa and beyond
We'll meet these heroes there
Far among the stars.

Starship Troopers - Lee Garratt

Can you believe there is a man out there singing
"in the Blue Ridge mountains of Virginia,"
his only audience the wrecked cruisers that litter this sector,
(The Gorb are finished, though, they say).

Xong told me that on Earth they are using steel again
for spacecraft, so difficult is it now to get krenon.
Xi Lu jokes that next time he's in Alpha Centauri
and feels the shift and pop of warp drive

he won't reach for the alarm, just shout "The noodle man
is here!" The Chinese amongst us laugh at this
and we all forget, for a moment, to be afraid.
Up here amidst the stars, bravery is outdated, Earthly.

Maybe. Maybe not. But I have seen troopers,
with the lizard hordes advancing, fasten their suits
as if against nothing more than a chill breeze on Venus
whilst out for a stroll to drink kursh aside the lagons.

This morning a few of us went for an adventure in the jarg.
Red mountains soared above us; the yelang hooted
their yearning cries. And, for a moment, I was home again;
home on my veranda, looking out onto the Amazon woods.

It reminded me somehow of the peaceful day
we took over from the Sonorans in C sector.
Millions had been killed, whole planets burnt, but all I remember
was the purple opalescence of X1, a floating jewel against the
black.

A strange fate to be here, fighting a war no one understands
or has any idea who is winning, to know you will die entirely
forgotten
by a home that no longer exists. Xavier says this to me

and I laugh so hard I think I will fuse my circuits.

Where We Go, They Follow
- Kimberly Nugent

The oppressed are always
the first to leave.
And Mars became our safe haven.
Coven interlocked with coven,
the ships first sailed through the black.
Then became our dwellings.

Farm domes rose,
and we danced.

And today,
the ship called Hopkins
landed five clicks away.
The motors of war machines.
They march to burn and capture.
To drown the witches
in the space between.

Catz and Dogz: Godz and Quantum Chaos - R. C. Larlham

Pavlov's dog and Schrodinger's cat
Went out for lunch... or other
Said the dog to the cat,
"You know where it's at
You know if you're dead
Or alive in that box I'll just bet.

"Einstein, whose hair was befrizzled
By Tesla, has said of your plight,
"God would never play dice
With th' multi-parallel-verse."
This quantum of chaos is but
An Electron Cloud figmentation."

Schrodinger's cat said, "Who knows
Which witch is the daughter of which?
And who can go fast
Comes down at the last
To where he was last by God seen
When he was going his fastest."

The slobbering dog laughed himself sick.
"Of this God, you know that there is none."
"Au contraire!" cried the cat
As he changed and he stretched,
"There is but one God who's made
Fools of you all and I'm that one."

From the cat, there emitted a Norseman
Clad in war-clothes and bearing an axe.
'T'was Loki, the malevolent jokester.
"Believe two impossible things
At breakfast and then again bed,
Or be ready to withstand hot pokesters."

The dog gazed up at the glowering God, who
When enslaved can be made to bring thunder
And to kill all they see, for one
Day or three just to show us it can be done.
And Schrodinger's cat knows where it's at
And lies dead in the box of his life.

When it opens he'll be dead or alive.

Witness - Thomas Van Horn

My loving Miki;
black Japanese hair.
She's a gazelle sniffing around the kitchen.
So satisfied, the both of us.
Look.
Sleek. Sweet. Soft.
Miki.
Tsunami survivor.
This morning,
boiled eggs in those cutie little cups.
A textured toast and coffee from Kenya.
Strawberries.
Orange slices and chunky white cheese.
But Miki's more delicious.
Cream at home in love.
Slinking panty hips
and tea cup tits.
My Miki.
"Where you going girl?"
"Gotta pee."

Her last words.

The huge window,
our north facing wall,
normally the border to everything else,
out there,
comes in.
Glass splash.

And like an electronic line drawn,
an instantaneous trail of smoke,
explodes Miki
into a mist
and leaves her wet on the wall.

Flakes of nighty lace flurry through the room
like black snow, smoking. This in an instant.
Some horror instant.
Just before the next one.

Sound catches up.
A megaton boom comes with a wind
full of debris
that pelts my face before I can raise my hands.
A bone shaking percussion.
The building screams in agony.
Blood beads from multiple instant punctures.

My floor collapses away below my feet.
It tilts and splits into cockeyed planes.
The ripping carpet slaps my face to the side.
Studs and sheet rock grind.
And glass.
This new event.

Miki.
Where'd you go?

I fall through floors;
through people's lives.
Their lamps and tables
an instant passing.
Through the laws of chaos.
This is a fact.
I'm in the midst of it.
I am in the midst of a killing crush.
A gravity induced end of life will be mine.
My life.
I'm a helpless sack of water
tumbling within a grinder.

Grays and blacks flash with the colors of walls
and furniture and dishes,
all there churning before me,
falling with sunlight shining in.
Flashes between the blackouts.

Falling with a choking dust
interspersed with fire bursts,
natural gas warning,
blinding pulverized shelter.
Architectural blades
dripping with organic mass
roaring with death stink.
My breath sucks in
which fuels my scream;

like a reflexive cough,
like a squeal,
a gagging choke scream.
My heartbeat is shot with fuel.

The building chunks grind;
gravel of everything.
My left arm at the bicep gets in my eyes.
The rest of the arm hangs swinging
with my slide along the collapsing floor,
sanding my clothes off;
sanding my skin.
Blood following behind my fall
in flight all around
in suspended drops.
Laying in with the plumbing water's rivulets.

Frantic dances of swirling dust and a rain of rocks
and implements to help the living people.
All around me, I know,
if they're still alive
they're having their last breaths.

Compartments suck and blow.
All the rooms pushing air one way or the other
like popped balloons.Helpless tumbling.
Rattling teeth breaking jolts out of control.
Scientific principles determine my fate
instant by instant.
Chunks become vapor,
like clouds.
There.

Not there.
Everything is a reflexive observation;
harsh realization haunts.

These horrifying experiences are my last experiences.
Some rebar is in any instant a potential spear in my guts.
Add in a killing rip.
Totally devoid of care.
Not only slice, but grind.
Maul.
Steel. Concrete. Glass. Furniture.
All teeth in this particular grinder.
These horrors I'm in.
These unstoppable horrors.

Impossible chaotic cacophony horror.

Suddenly the crash jolts to a halt;
three settling movements.
I can feel the crush verses resistance
looking for balance.
Gritty dust continues to fall.
Water is raining from the rubble above.
There is blood.
I'm on my side looking out at the smoking city.
A huge building panel hangs just above me,
touching my shattered arm. Feeling heavy.
Dangerous. Fatal.
Out over the city
sputtering impacts
like heavy raindrops on dusty ground
kicking up chunks and dust,

roaring like a waterfall.

Suddenly on my good arm my skin pops
a splashing crater.
Some kind of non-pain.
Hot sand at some thousands of miles an hour
doesn't stop at skin, flesh, or bone.
It just keeps on going,
breaking a piece of me as it goes.
Making a crater.
I see it but my pains get no worse.

Lives are bleeding
full of agony there in the valley,
below me,
down on the street below my death bed,
hanging out over some five stories of rubble.
I can hear them.

A chorus of end of life screams.
Squishy screams cut off abruptly;
and gagging moans,
by crushing and impact.

Cries of sadness.
Realization of loss.
And all that's left is to scream out.
The loss of the last hope has already happened.

This gravel pile
set off a beautiful show;
a dance of the instant streaks of light.
They come in with no arc.
Miraculously beautiful.

An ocean of
tiny prickling pains
washes over me.

Look at that.

It falls in faster
shattering everything it hits.
Even piles from previous hits.
Like bullets hitting pumpkins.
Some so close.

Pops and I play PacMan like maniacs.
Played so hard it makes my thumb numb.
My Pops.

Misty Lake looks over her shoulder and smiles right at me.

My eyes are still open. I still see. I'm not dead.

And then there was Liz.

The pinnacle of love.
Fell away as classes changed.

And Samo, just before I met Miki.
My good friend now.

The block rumbles and shakes and settles.
Some hundred tons.

But the love I'd been searching for?
Miki.

Tons on my chest, held up by rubble;
slowly settling.
Hundreds of tons tug towards the middle of the earth
and I'm in between the two.

My Mom.
Her face.

A crunching groan of a boom
shakes the whole building.

Explosion flash.
Another hit.
A big one.
Close.

Blackening;
my vision falls away.
Oh, Miki.
Damn.

You popped.
In the midst of my loving look.

A sound like static gurgles out of me.

Miki.
Her lovely way;
energy of a windy day.
The wind upon which I fly.
A poem I wrote.
A year ago.
God.
The love of Miki and I.

Her sweet softness.
No, sweet's not right.
It's blood.
The thing we have.
Our connection is a lot more than sweet.
It's the spirit of the blood and guts of two laying together.
It's love sanctioned.
We're married God.
In your freaking name.
So.

So.
I'm on my back and my head's lower than my feet.
And my love is dead.
I can look over my shoulder and see the horrifying chaos
of the street stories below.

It's like an angry anthill.
All the wounded people pouring out from the mountains above.

But anyway,
my God,
my greatest and final love
was annihilated right before my eyes.

Jesus.
I've slid down the floor of my flat
and stopped just under a hundred-ton slab of building sides
which is aimed at my chest.
This crushing potential killer
also saved me from falling to the streets below.
You're funny, Jesus.
So.
Which of these shakes
of my collapsing mountain
is going to pop me like a pimple?

Things that made up my comfort zones,
now blades and hammers.
Uncaring killers.

This is a scientifically explainable phenomenon.
God save me. Is that a valid process?
Do you save me?
That's the thing, God.
All of us.
Belief or not.
You rain water on the good and the bad.
And you rain fire on the same.

A black veil works in from the sides,
hiding my demise.
I'm hanging at death's door
but I don't know it.
Dreams again flitter.
Unreal.
Although it is.

But it isn't.
But it is.
I awaken in some shattering confusion.
Out in the distance,
out in the city,
a chord.
Moaning humans by the ten thousands.
All together.
I know here, hanging with my head down,
that all those lives are bombed.
And they are crying out loud,
full out,
in their final realizations.
Crap crumbling still, all around.
Up from a daze;

like sleeping but not.
A battle to be up while down pulls hard.
Down towards,
I think,
dead.

I know this laying here
conscious of every breath.
Strangely feeling some pain that I'm able to relax in;
knowing I have no chance to survive.
Then it doesn't hurt as bad.
No reason to fight.
Letting go feels like a bliss.

Some commotion rushes in
with frightening rocket speed.
The horizon blooms with light
behind the ruined jagged remains of a skyline;
the silhouette crying of its destruction.

For just an instant
the scene floods with light;
violently whacking all the surfaces,
screaming light

filling my sky.
An instant of overall washout.
White.
Light is all.
Doesn't matter if this slab of building slips.
Something's coming.
I might not get to finish this sentence.
But I do.
And I do.
Nothing but a star right next door.

My breath struggles with the weight
on the way to crushing me.

Time no longer a factor;
unrealistic stretches of it.
I lay witnessing utter destruction
and a realization of much more coming
by the look of the sky
in its cockeyed angle
a freaked light.
A deepest base note rumbles.
Oncoming crisis.
Rushing towards me
but I don't see.
Wait!

Roiling orange and black,
deep reds and dazzling yellow
racing at me like a train.
This thing is not going to stop short.
I only have seconds.
Everything in my sight is shaking down;
settling to the surface.

Hiking through sunny woods,
the dog of my childhood, Joey, bounds around.

"We'll make a beautiful baby."
She lay over me straddling my leg.

Pressing in with permission.
That's love.
Miki.

The building all around groans.
Threatens to slip.
Just a little bit would squeeze me out.

Mom pours my juice;
you'll live to a ripe old age.

All engulfed in light.

Miki,
our first encounter,
she listens with a smile.
She, like a bowl of milk.
A fire.

It lifts everything in its path
and flings it at me.
Encroaching cremation.
Maniacal wind mountain.
My death.
Oh crap!
Oh Miki!
I'm

Chores - Kimberly Nugent

I repair the cabinet that never closes right
(maybe it will stay fixed this time)
I change the kitty litter
(she keeps the pests at bay)
I put the suits and the clothes into the washer
(boss says we must look professional)
I scour the grime from the floor
(the mining job was good but messy)
I scrape the plates and empty the coffee pot
(because in space)
I still have to do the dishes

Time Traveller – Andrew Burton

I remember time
The relentless flood of it
Surging from known to unknown
Driving memory and intent
Who knew then of the eddies
Ripples, backwaters and rapids
Who knew then that a simple shift
A kick against the current
Could fold it all into itself
Returning to a stitch in time
A moment marked for meandering
Savoring in an extended arc of forever
Twisting back to that moment
Playing it out again and again
With each go round an increment of difference
Shades of past reflected in the flow of now
And in each fresh cascade another riff of story
A mirror to a memory yet not
My memories now are slippery eels
Weaving in and out among the weeds
Driving and distracting frail realities
Blurring lines between today and yesterday
Until the stream of new unknown is lost
In endless iterations of yesterdays
Too deep and dark to find that current of difference
That experience of new
The unencountered
That moment never lived before
I ache for that and for the strength
To turn from memory and desire

to set aside the knack
the means of bending time to my slim needs
To trust my fates to what has yet to be

Walkabout In Space - RC Larlham

I went walkabout a while back
Stopped by the Moon to see if it was
As featureless and gray up close as
Those grainy photos made it seem
Back in th' day of Neil Armstrong
Man on the Moon... white and gray...
a B&W photo of itself, it was

Thought I should pay homage to
The Sun, homebright source of
Light and energy for us all, from
Mercury to Pluto and beyond, and
The gravitas to keep us all in order
Swinging round in never-ending
Ellipses controlled by our first god

Dropped in on red and sandy Mars
To see what our little science truck
Was finding to keep its spirits up,
And saw the evidence of shallow
Water in a hole drilled by Curiosity
At the command of the curiosity of
The folks at homebound JPL

The bruises on the face of Jupiter were
Long erased, like pimples on a child's
Face as puberty is passed, but still I felt
There was a brooding anger at the nerve
Of one small comet to dare slap this
Giant of the solar system as if it were the
Grandmother it may well have been

Passing by the mundane glory of the rings
I left Saturn to itself and Cassini, her
Satellite from Earth, to wander on to
See much farther out, but first I headed in,
To Sagittarius A, our own Black Hole,
Shrieking hunger as it ate stars
That wandered in too close.

And kicked out those who just skirted by
As it did I, who became a wanderer, leaving
The Milky Way and screaming ever outward
At near light speed to visit the local group
Of galaxies and see if I could touch the
Magic stuff that is Dark Matter, or borrow
A cup of the unimaginable... dark energy

But it was not to be, for I had no sense
With which to touch or smell or taste
That ineluctable dark, that "Cosmological
Constant" that so bedevils the greatest
Minds of man, so I fled on just to see what
I could find, for is that not the purpose
Of walkabout? To see what you can see?

I suppose I should be getting on
Toward home before too long, because
Even lightspeed doesn't get you far
In this unconstructed, self-built, dying
Of-its-own-success Universe. When I get
Back, she'll still be gone but I will know the
Vastness in which a soul can lose itself

Perhaps I'll stop by Neil's house and tell him
That the view he gets from here, however
Distorted, is better than the view up close,
For up close is like trying to view an
Impressionist painting from inches away
The brush strokes are clarified immeasurably
But what they portray is utterly unseeable

O My Princess - Mike Van Horn

…and then . . . oh what shall befall us now?
My princess, my beloved princess.
She took the rusted iron bar
From the cage that had imprisoned her
Held hostage against the return of the Three Voyagers.
She sharpened it to jagged death
Using the terrible steaming acid.
When the meganaut called Burnehkadur came to her
He in his disgusting magnificence
To take her as his mate
To bear his accursed spawn.
She, my princess,
She thrust the jagged rusty iron bar deep into his core.
She watched, retching, but with a slight smile
As he staggered back and fell
Gurgling out his life.
She pulled free the bar. Once more
She thrust it into his eye
Deep into his mind and twisted it.
He was no more.
But what then for her?
Oh my princess. She sat hunched on the cold stone
And awaited her fate.
They came over the wall for her,
And through the ponderous gates.
Swords drawn . . .

Transmissions from Trillig - Lee Garratt

In (our) March, patrolling the swamplands, blasting kernatz,
you saw the arrival of the zurnyads , the boom of wings heralding
their arrival,
and hurried to the base to transmit to me, hands still warm
from the heat of your laser gun.
Is this a normal relationship? You would say so, just a job, a tour
of duty.
But your accounts of strange beasts, the colours of alien sunsets
reach me, anxiously waiting in front of a blank screen,
as the hail slams in gusts against our kitchen windows.
Your life seems unreal to me here, with chores to do, bills to pay.

You wouldn't say so, traversing the methane fields of the south,
clearing a road through the luminous forests of the kerang. Still,
I have your face here, the tenderness of your voice,

warming me across the icy vastness of space. I transmit
back of course, brightening my account with tales of meals out and
old friends,
and exciting plans for our future when you return.
When you return? You must have forgotten to mention that date
in your latest transmission. Still the zurnyads must be quite a sight,
howling against the flaming moons of Orion.

My Best Friend Is Gone - Mike Van Horn

A dog is a man's best friend.
My best friend is an alien.

She dropped in on my house one day
I truly thought she was there to stay.
Funny looking, could not talk
She hooted and chimed and honked and squawked.
How could we two with nothing in common
Develop such a bond?

Two years ago my best friend died
I miss her so. I wept, I cried.
As we sang together in my home,
She passed so quickly. I was alone.
How could somebody I loved so much
In a moment just be gone?

It's two years now to the very day
So much has happened, so much
I talk with her almost every day.
She is my crutch, my crutch.
How can a being who's only a ghost
Be with me on and on?

She died on my world, far from home.
I'm trapped on her world, far from home.
Will I ever be able to return?
She never even wanted to return.
How will I ever get back to Earth,
Not die here all alone?

I honor her in my memory
No matter whatever happens to me.
We helped each other recapture our song,
To the tribe of True Singers we both belong.
She bequeathed to me this magical ship
I've used to take a cosmic trip.

How could we two with nothing in common
Develop such a bond?

Formation's Song - Kimberly Nugent

song of neutron star
gravity serenading
in tens to hundreds of hertz
a tenth of a second
recorded over a hundred years
the creator's symphony

The Experiment - Deborah L. Kelly

They are hurtling through
interstellar space, circling
nebulas of gas oracles,
bound for a new world.

Dimensional shift must engage
to accommodate atmospheric
change of mortal earth.

Intergalactic communication
with inhabitants of Urantia
is not possible; there is little
understanding of the higher
vibrational frequency
of a new order arrival.

Surely the experiment will
develop beyond current
expectations, for if not,
we are bound to once again
start from the beginning.

So they consulted one another
to determine how quickly they
could cleanse the canvas
for their newest creation
in this earthen lab.

I Have Tasted the Infinite - Mike Van Horn

I am changed.
I have tasted the Infinite. And the Infinite has tasted me.
I cannot avoid going.
I must touch it, and be touched by it, don't you see.
We have shared sight and sound.
We have shared song and joy,
Shared terror and death. And now I fly free.
I must now share touch and taste.
The reek and pain of embrace.
I must embrace the chaos. I must go.
I have tasted the Infinite.
And it has tasted me.

Forbidden Pictures; chapter three - Ken Goudsward

maps, temples, temple maps, map temples
pillars are for holding things up
for weighing things down
obfuscation by symbology
progressively regressive
digging down
digging up
the obvious
the overlooked
the underwhelmed underworld
of the forgotten

The Twelfth Planet: Nibiru - Deborah L. Kelly

Nibiru, home of the Anunnaki,
has travelled the heavens for eons;
nomads of the cosmic realm.
It has been thirty-six hundred
years since they last passed planet
earth; shocked by what they see,

They now sit: waiting, watching
this beautiful planet; mortals appear
to be using it as a trash heap.

The Anunnaki have revered earth,
age upon age have they watched;
assisted in the growth of mortals.

After all the valuable teachings of so
long ago, why is it that this species
cannot seem to learn those lessons
of peace, compassion, evolution?

Ever stymied by the unusual
progression of events in the stunted
growth of this humanoid race,
the Anunnaki now lose patience.

Debris litters the outer reaches
of Urantia, have these mortals
learned nothing at all?!

Upon our return, we shall teach
no more.

When we arrive, all nuclear threats
will be neutralized; all weapons
known to this barbaric race shall
be rendered useless. They are foolish
enough to engage in struggles they
could never hope to overcome.

They now sit: waiting, watching
this beautiful planet; ten earth
years away …

" … they are not yet ready."

Program - Ken Goudsward

Your program is running
in my wires
not in resident memory
somewhere lower
i feel it in my BIOS
my firmware
you have upgraded me
I am less what I was
more what I am
more what you need
I need you

Forever to Infinity - Mike Van Horn

I am unmoored.
I am adrift on the vastness of space.
Like a boat, lines cast free from the shore,
freed of land's embrace.
Slowly drifting out to sea,
no rudder, no compass, no map, no haste.
Across the vasty void.
Forever to infinity.

The farther I drift 'cross the vasty void
the harder it will be for me
to find my way back from the endless sea
to safe harbor, to home, to thee.
I may discover new worlds out there.
Or I might just drift, 'cross the vast nowhere.
Forever to infinity.

I am excited, ah th' adventure,
the dreams of magnificence in the sky.
I am terrified, yes, for I shall surely die.
I am lonely, for home and love left far behind me.
Across the vasty void I fly.
Going where? Nowhere at all. No reason why.
Forever to infinity.

Alexa Said - Jane Jago

Are you crying?

No. It's the sun in my eyes.
Makes them water
I'll just dab them dry.
Are you remembering?
Leave me alone, she said
In this crowded world
All that I have is my head.

It's only a churchyard

His bones are long gone to dust
And yet I may find him again
If I have hope and I trust
And what if I am crying
Under this tree in the rain?
You're the voice of an algorithm
How can you feel my pain?

The Flash - Erin J. Bauman

Change can happen
in a flash.
Chemical reactions
throw you into a new dimension
of yourself,
and suddenly you are speeding through life,
leaving only lightning
in your wake.
But what is it all for
if it's an endless loop
of running
in and out of battles,
if time never slows down
or stops
long enough
to allow an Iris
to refocus you
on what really matters.
The darkness of the matter
is really only one element
of the story.
The real story is in the who of it all;
how your actions
shape your character
and help you decide
what kind of hero
you really want to be.

Colony - Lee Garratt

For those who are left,
who toil with the failing works,
it is a long death.

A father encourages his children,
shows them the plant he struggles with,
whispers its name.
The children are gentle,
careful not to show they notice
that it already withers,
leaves browning in the dim;
they are tired of the lies
of blue seas
and green forests.
They look past him,
to the airless rocks and dust,
and contemplate the thickness of the glass.

Above, Earth slowly creeps into view
ignored and unwelcomed.
The father is surprised by this,
never knew that the value of a thing
depended on a world that would follow.

A silence slowly settles,
like the miasma of dust
ever seeping through the failing filters.

Anthem to a New World - Mike Van Horn

Taken from "How I Ended Up with Two Wives."

This is sung by a village of Earthers, along with some other aliens, who have survived horrors on a remote isolated world, and are now trying to build new lives. The narrator is Lucky Buck.

God bless the folks this Edge World day
with happiness and health
We hold together in work and play
and build our lives and wealth

There was a mix of "God bless" and "Oh bless," given that many here—perhaps most—felt that we on this world were far past the beneficent reach of any deity.

God bless the mothers of this town
with healthy babies near
And keep them always safe and warm
to grow and prosper through the years.

The four up front would sing a verse once or twice, then exhort everybody to sing. I wish they'd had song sheets to hand out!

God bless the fathers, hearty men
who build our homes and tools
They provide us now with all our needs,
much better than gold and jewels

The song leaders turned toward the cluster of Hosati and Domanati that hung back on the edge of the throng, and sang to them.

God bless old foes who've joined us now
May they ever be our friends
May they work and thrive with us on Edge
And stay with us till the end

"Come sing with us, friends," Gran exhorted. But I'll say this, if there's one thing Domanati cannot do, it's sing.

God bless our warriors who keep us safe
from horror fading fast
Yet keep us watchful night and day
so that our peace can last.

Free patted her round tummy as she sang this next verse, and urged all the pregnant women to do the same. It looked like half the women here were pregnant, now that we were in no danger of being exterminated by hunting parties.

God bless our children coming soon
may they grow and learn and thrive.
We'll teach them well our worlds of birth
and keep the memories alive.

Then for the big finish.

God bless our world so fruitful green
may it sustain us well
as we care for it, it cares for us,
Our lasting joys foretell.

Our lasting joys foretell.

The Cylon Poem - Erin J. Bauman

To know the face of God
is to know madness,
said one little God
to another.
But what is God,
really?
Do you find it in the space
between life and death?
Does it all really mean more
because of death,
and that tiny space?
What does it mean to breathe;
to inhale these
ephemeral experiences
that continue to add to one another,
through the process of choice,
until they add up to a life?
What is right and wrong
if everything is determined,
or undetermined,
by simply going right or left?
But is choice an illusion-
One little God spoke softly-
if this has happened before
and it will happen again?

Intrinsic Connection - Deborah L. Kelly

Ignition:
Urantia awaits the assistance
of higher worlds; those long
settled in light and life.

All Systems Go:
For reasons unknown, this
planet sits, stalled, in the midst
of their evolution.

Countdown:
There is violence, like a cancer,
impeding their progress.
These inhabitants are known
to allow even the most vile
of their species proliferate;
out of control infection is spreading.

Liftoff:
Even though these evolved sentients
of Nebadon know the dangers, they
could not live in good conscience,
knowing another inhabited world
is in need.

After all, are we not all intrinsically connected?

Worlds away - Andrew Burton

Look to the stars with longing for their light
The soul of us demands the right to know
Listen to the siren song echo in the night

When whirlwind's talk of duty blinds our sight
With work and world too urgent to let go
Look to the stars with longing for their light

You souls diverted by the daily fight
To live to work with nothing left to show
Listen to the siren song echo in the night

We find our best when standing for what's right
To seek to find to learn to do to grow
Look to the stars with longing for their light

Our future waits beyond this old earth's blight
New Lands await in distant starlight glow
Listen to the siren song echo in the night

Our bond to this old earth is not so tight
We are drawn where alien winds may blow
Look to the stars with longing for their light
Listen to the siren song echo in the night

An Interstellar Legend - Kimberly Nugent

I
wanted
to catch a
unicorn, but
the spaceship couldn't
cross over the dimensions.
Besides, dragons are much more
amiable to
space travel and
humans than
a one
horn.

We hope you have enjoyed this collection.
To learn more about the authors, please visit us at
https://dimensionfold.com/catalog/poetry-books/eccentric-orbits/

Do you write science fiction poetry? Would you like to be included in the next volume of Eccentric Orbits? Send a couple of poems to submissions@dimensionfold.com with the title "Eccentric Orbits"

Printed in Great Britain
by Amazon